REMNANTS OF A FULL MOON

MICHELLE GONZALEZ

LOS ANGELES † NEW YORK † LONDON † MELBOURNE

Remnants of a Full Moon by Michelle Gonzalez
ISBN: 978-1-947240-82-7 Paperback
ISBN: 978-1-947240-83-4 eBook

Copyright © 2023 Michelle Gonzalez . All rights reserved.
First Printing 2023
Cover art by Dennis Callaci
Layout and design by Mark Givens

For information:
Bamboo Dart Press
chapbooks@bamboodartpress.com

Bamboo Dart Press 039

www.pelekinesis.com

www.bamboodartpress.com

SHRiMPER
www.shrimperrecords.com

For Jesse and Zoey

CONTENTS

Relics

When an Introvert Tries to Mingle 8
Mom's Favorite Painting 9
You Handed Me a Promise Ring................................ 10
Jesse at 20 11
Remnants of a Full Moon 12
Go with Grace 13
On Hearing a similar Experience
    (at 12 years old)... 14
No Rain on Sunday.. 15
Small Climbs 16
On Being Fearful 17
On Telling My Daughter That Daddy is Sick 18
A Church Sign 19
On Leaving the Door Locked 20

What Remains

Nightly Routines 22
A Swim in Early Summer 23
Revisiting the Phone at Night 24
On Needing Coffee 25
Mock Affection 26
Book 27

Stuffed Friend 28
You Don't Like to Play, Do You? 29
A Number Lonelier Than One 30
San Xavier 31
Continental Divide 32
Stalactites 33
Patiently Waiting 34
1992 Revisited 35
On Seeing the Green Pool 36
End of Summer 37
While She Works 38
Creator 39
Here Rests 40
Catastrophe 41
Awkward Afternoon 42
Another Morning Moon 43

RELICS

WHEN AN INTROVERT TRIES TO MINGLE

What a delight,
I proved that I fit in a gym locker.

My hands not even
touching the top,
my back not even
having to bend.

The inside not completely
filled with lackluster.

It is actually comforting,
the familiar smell of my books
that wait for me
during my required physical education.

I will give it a moment before
I ask to be let out of the locker,
then I will smile and wave
as I walk past the person
that questioned my height.

MOM'S FAVORITE PAINTING

Her favorite painting
is the one
with the little girl
In a baby-doll dress.
Her nose in the corner of the room
without a chair to sit on.

The girl waits for approval
to leave the spot.

I'm sure she was told
to think about the reason
she is standing there
although I am not sure
she even knows why.

The dog standing beside her
seems to empathize,
his nose also in the corner.

Maybe my mom sees a little of herself
in the defiant little girl.
Surely it is not me that she sees.

YOU HANDED ME A PROMISE RING

That was enough
for me to believe you.
To calm
the questioning owl.

Whispered promise to me
before I closed your
blue car door
for the last time.

Your voice quiet.
Nervousness in your eyes,
repeating the promise
you said was just between us.

Said promise
and I held on to it,
as if it were a
fragile buttercup
waiting for its chance
to be exposed to
the light.

JESSE AT 20

Bless this guy born with
the wires in his heart reversed.
Who threw a snowball at me
after jumping in the snow
not knowing what was beneath.
Saturdays we would drive
with no conversation,
only the radio playing
on high volume
making my ears numb.
Turning, he would look
and check to see if I was still there.
On the nights that I worked late,
he stood guard at the door
of the restaurant
locking it once we closed.
He drove me home after
and made sure I locked
the door behind.
He looks the same as then
but now he watches the news
with his hair that has hints
of silver in it.

REMNANTS OF A FULL MOON

The last full moon in October
that I remember
was thirteen years ago.
A strong-willed child
came into the world
three weeks early.
Now, on this full moon
another strong-willed child
who is five years old
decides to not stand in line or
sit cross-legged on the classroom carpet.

On this full moon
she finds it hard to explain
why she can't practice self-control
and I wonder what the new moon will bring.

GO WITH GRACE

She no longer looks nervous
as we walk towards the school gate
on this cool winter morning.

She has already told me that
Phil has predicted
six more weeks of winter.

This however,
is not what is on my mind.

Images of ventilators
and sounds of coughing
fill my head.

I keep my composure
as she adjusts her mask
while walking towards
her first-grade class.

ON HEARING A SIMILAR EXPERIENCE
(AT 12 YEARS OLD)

A friend looked at me funny
when I told her stories
of how one night
there would yelling before bed
then the next night
goodnights and I love you.
The sound of arguing
my safety and security.
There was also not knowing
if I would ride the bus to school
the next day.
I also wanted to be dropped off
with a hug and homemade lunch.

Some Saturdays we would go
to confession,
only to repeat the offenses
the following week.

My friend told me that her mom
would enjoy a drink on most evenings
while her dad stayed busy in the garage.

I told her,
this seems typical to me.

NO RAIN ON SUNDAY

I complain as I drive in the rain
on the way to morning drop off.

I do not enjoy the feeling of rain drops
on my face,
or the dampness
that causes my hair to frizz.

Two days later
on the seventh day of the week,
the sun shines
over the freeway exit.

There are no rain drops as I walk
towards the church.

Just like the week before.

SMALL CLIMBS

She asks if we can go for a walk
after school.
Although I do not have the energy
to climb the small hill
I agree to her request.

My breathing staggers at the top of the hill
where we see my parents' house.

We walk past admiring the red roses
and the thick green grass.
She carefully grabs a lemon from
the thorny tree.

When my dad comes outside,
he talks about the weather and tells us of his
current project of planting and watering.

The house hasn't changed
since our first walk,
I sometimes wonder
what the house will look like
a few years from now
when we take a small climb.

ON BEING FEARFUL

The boy coughs
as his mother tells him
to cover his mouth.

Another woman on her cell phone
says she is not sick as she sneezes.

The number of people increases,
masks covering their mouths and noses.

Voice of the man echoes instructions.

Thoughts of the mother,
she'd rather it was her that was sick
and not her child.

Hearing moans and conversations of others,
picturing a quiet room and quiet house,
where the child will no longer play.

ON TELLING MY DAUGHTER THAT DADDY IS SICK

Your dimple filled smile
is your most infectious thing.

I want it to be triggered by
music that makes you
do an impromptu dance routine.
Turning your steps into a cartwheel
ending with a fashionable pose.
Afterwards waiting for your audience
of stuffed animals to respond.

Not this burden
of waiting until Daddy
is no longer in isolation or solitude,
in this moment filled with the uncertain.

I too cannot wait
until there is no more
distance between us.
We silently pray for that day.

A CHURCH SIGN

The sign once read
"Time to come to church".
On my way to the store
I noticed the weathered sign with a white background
and faded letters.

I wondered if children still played
on the metal slide
and small climbing structure
made of wood that has begun to splinter.

On a recent trip to the store
I notice that they have replaced the sign
and also added a sandbox.
I also notice the fresh black pavement
in the parking lot.

I imagine this was a result of many nights of devotion.

ON LEAVING THE DOOR LOCKED

I reach for my keys to open the classroom.
As soon as it opens I turn the knob
back to the locked position.
I do not remember
the last time the door
remained unlocked.

I glance at the black lock that was installed
and remember the students asking
the proper procedure if we should hear
the discharge of a gun.

I think of my daughter's teacher
explaining to the students
that they need to hide and remain quiet
if they hear an unfamiliar boom.
She then tells her class that she will be the hen
protecting her little chicks.
She then says they should throw rocks
at the bad person and run for safety if need be.

I process this when my daughter tells me
and I wait to cry until she is fast asleep.

WHAT REMAINS

NIGHTLY ROUTINES

She says, "Daddy, will you dry my hair?"
I listen as they laugh.
They have caught the dog's attention.
They pretend to dry his hair
as he barks at the blow dryer.

Afterwards, she asks for her hair to be brushed.
So her dad brushes from top to bottom
while having a conversation
about her future car she will drive.
I see a grin form at the side of his mouth
as I try to remember if my dad ever brushed my hair.

I wonder if he fears
that she will not remember
their nightly routines that start
while I drive home from work.

A SWIM IN EARLY SUMMER

Her toes touch the water
and she exaggerates as she explains
that the water is cold.

On the first step she pauses and shivers
then she takes another step,
shrieking as she inches down the ladder
even though the temperature is the same.

She refuses to jump in,
the idea causing her fear
and she retreats back to the second step.

Once she is in
I begin the same process.
My body feeling the same sensation
as my toes touch the same water.

I won't tell her that
her exaggeration was warranted.

REVISITING THE PHONE AT NIGHT

My eyes open
as I reach for the phone.
I look at the time and
I feel a pain in my chest
and notice my shallow breaths.

My phone lights up,
I see the time.
3am, the witching hour.
Do they even call it that anymore?

If feels a little different this time.
Not like the time when my arms refused
to cooperate with my thoughts.
My legs remained still as well.

I do not hear the sound of lullabies
coming from the other room.
Then the sound of the dog softly panting
begins to fill my ears.
The music also starts to become clear
and I hope that this will help me
fall to sleep as well.

ON NEEDING COFFEE

Cartoons play loudly
on the television
at seven in the morning.
First, she asks for a cup of milk
then she asks for cereal,
sometimes asking for apple juice as well.
As she explains the plot of the show
I nod and pretend I understand
the characters' motivations.

I feel a slight sense of irritation.

As the dog demands food and attention,
the irritation turns into anger.
He wags his tail as I pick up his food dish.

Passing the coffee maker,
I realize the origin of my bitterness.
I return to the living room a few minutes later,
coffee in hand and eyes no longer blurry.

She doesn't say a word as we sit in silence.
Then I ask questions and become intrigued
by the colorful television screen.
My irritation turns into curiosity
as the cup warms my hands.

MOCK AFFECTION

He is not a human I tell you,
he is a canine with fur
that sheds on the carpet.

He annoys me
like an insistent mosquito
that longs to feed on my blood.

And the constant seeking
of attention and petting,
which I thought only cats requested.

His eyes asking for forgiveness
after he relieves himself on the kitchen floor.
I am not fooled.
I know those eyes are deceiving,
a defense mechanism.
His wide brown eyes looking to soothe
the anger that I refuse to let go of.
Only once when I saw his body convulsing
did I feel sympathetic.
Who knew dogs could be epileptic?
How can I be content when there's another
soul in the house,
that doesn't know
he is not a human?

BOOK

Blazing Summertime
the excellent, small book hides
into the shadows.

STUFFED FRIEND

Depressing nighttime
a favorite, big toy loves
at the perfect time.

YOU DON'T LIKE TO PLAY, DO YOU?

She asks as she prepares to run across the lawn.
I give her a look and she changes her tone.
She then says, "You like to read and write, don't you?"

How do I explain that I find joy
in watching her count
and play hide and seek
with her canine companion?
How do I tell her
I marvel as she practices
walking on her hands
until she gets it right?

My smile is on the inside,
and I clap in my mind.

A NUMBER LONELIER THAN ONE

I found a number lonelier than one.
Perhaps the number three is envious
of the number one and two,
smiling and laughing
but not turning
to see if number three is still there.

Three is not part of the jokes and smile.
She is holding the camera
documenting the private moments
between one and two.

SAN XAVIER

On a Friday afternoon
I walk into what remains
of the Spanish mission
in southern Arizona.
Organ music plays
to fill the silence
of the room
full of people praying.
I wonder if behind the masked faces
they seek forgiveness
or intervention
on a family member's behalf.

I wait and watch
while some worship
and others respectfully
take in the history
in silent awe.

CONTINENTAL DIVIDE

Somewhere atop
the continental divide
12,095 feet above,
the clouds slowly
begin to release
droplets of rain.

In the middle of June
the temperature has dropped
to 56 degrees.
I feel unprepared as
I search for a sweater
to cover my summer outfit.

We imagine the mountain tops
that are in the view
are covered with snow
and the roads
covered with ice.

I am grateful for this cool relief,
unlike the desert
hundreds of miles away
where we call home.

STALACTITES

Icicle like minerals
hang from the ceiling
in the cave that is
dimly lit.

Our eyes adjust
as we look at the various
shapes and sizes.
One looks like a small
Russian puppet theater,
others look like fingers
about to touch.
He explains to our daughter
that this was many years in the making.

My favorite is the one she pointed out
and we make our hands
into the shape of a heart to replicate
the formation.
How many years
did it take to make
this tender form?

PATIENTLY WAITING

They imagine him
sitting at the door
waiting for us to return
from our week long excursion.

They imagine his confusion
as we did not return
on the first night.

I wonder,
did he howl at the moon
or bark all night?
Our family members tell us otherwise.

When we return he jumps
in disbelief and then sleeps through
the night.

1992 REVISITED

My dad sits in the lobby
of the urgent care
with memories of
doctors intervening
to find the cause of his bleeding
and telling him
his liver will not function
for much longer.

He remembers transfusions
and needles
along with the sounds
of machines beeping
late into the morning.

When he is finally called into the room
he tells the doctor
this has happened before
in 1992.

He is one step closer
to accepting his impermanency
days before his sixty-sixth birthday.

ON SEEING THE GREEN POOL

She asks to go for another swim
but the pool has managed
to turn a faint hint of green
yet again.

We were unable to keep
the water clear and smelling
of fresh chemicals.

We hope next year
will be the year
that we manage to have
clear water.

Perhaps we will even
keep the grapefruit tree that is near the pool
from wilting away.

If not,
we can blame
the excruciating heat.

END OF SUMMER

We don't walk our dog
at 8:00pm,
after the sun has gone down
on a 100-degree day.

Our dog is too excitable
and doesn't know how
to socialize with others.

He once urinated on company
after smelling the scent
of a female dog
on someone's pants.

And we don't go out
on a trip for ice cream
once it is dark outside.

We usually start
the nightly routine
well before eight at night
in hopes of getting
the required amount of sleep
after the child has gone to bed.

WHILE SHE WORKS

If she was at home this evening,
she would see him prepare
the ingredients he needs
to make their dinner.

Deciding on a tray of enchiladas,
he carefully fried the tortillas
then dipped them in the red sauce.
Afterwards, he placed the cheese in the middle
before rolling the hot tortilla while burning
his fingers like when she makes them.

If she could hear him,
she would catch him asking
why she continues to work
and leave their house they have lived in
for over thirty years.

If she would speak
she would say to him,
let's forget about the dishes
and go watch the sunset elsewhere.

CREATOR

A wide-eyed girl
born in the month
of thankfulness,
carefully reads the instructions
on her new set of Legos.
Her face covered in concentration
as she begins to follow them.

Of course, she is precise.
Isn't that the way she was taught?
Eventually she will have to follow other instructions.

This is not her creation,
it is an exercise
in patience and learning.

In a few days
the set will be taken apart
and put back into pieces.

Later she will refer
to the instructions
when she wants to rebuild the set,
but wouldn't she prefer
to make her own creations?

HERE RESTS

Your grandmother
born many years ago,
who carried
her faith with her.

While she was passing,
her husband and children gathered
in the small welcoming house
that she would
clean daily.

Her sons quiet,
while her daughters
wept.

The bible by the
side of her bed
remains,
it will no longer
be read by her.

Today the room
is silent with respect,
and her consecrated assignment
now complete.

CATASTROPHE

She woke up late
and still asks for cartoons
and cereal.
You do not hear her.
Now she wants to
play with the dog
as she twirls in the living room.

We will definitely
catch the train when
we cross the bridge
just before the school.

A few minutes later he calls
to say the dog is being clingy
and his coworkers are incompetent
already, at eight in
the morning.

I reach work,
emails and students
are waiting.

Patience will be required today.
Grab my Bible and favorite verse.
Go out praying.

AWKWARD AFTERNOON

I'm glad you find my awkwardness entertaining.
You laughed as I tried to figure out
how to hold the cape that will protect me
as you take the x-rays.

And when I sit in the examination chair,
there is a question of where to place my hands.

I usually just fold them
politely in my lap.

When the dentist looks into my mouth
I wonder if it is rude to make eye contact.
I also wonder if they think I'm asleep
as I close my eyes.

When they are finished
I say thank you.

Is that the proper protocol
after someone has inflicted pain?

ANOTHER MORNING MOON

Another early October morning
with clouds covering the haze.

The moon still visible
and appearing to be full.

She notices and points it out
on the drive to school.
There is excitement in her voice.

She does not know
that in a few weeks,
she will lose her
first canine
and beloved friend.

She is not prepared
for the void that it will bring.

ABOUT THE AUTHOR

Michelle Gonzalez is a native of southern California and is the author of five chapbooks of poetry, including *Morning in the House by the Field* and *Wild Chrysanthemum*. Her work has also appeared in various anthologies such as *The GNU Literary Journal*, *Writing From Inlandia* anthologies, and *San Bernardino, Singing*.

Michelle teaches Language Arts in the local school district. She continues to write about her experiences in the Inland Empire where she lives with her family.

112 N. Harvard Ave. #65
Claremont, CA 91711
chapbooks@bamboodartpress.com
www.bamboodartpress.com

www.ingramcontent.com/pod-product-compliance
Lightning Source LLC
Chambersburg PA
CBHW080943040426
42444CB00015B/3427